This book was compiled by Daniel Melehi
with the A.I assistance of Inventabot

Dedication

I hope this helps all of my wonderful
readers achieve all their goals in their
business. And I would like to thank my
wonderful wife for all of her continued
support in all my ventures.

©Daniel Melehi

May 7 2023

Contents

Chapter 1: Understanding the Gig Economy................7

Subchapter 1.1: Defining the Gig Economy.................7

Subchapter 1.2: History and Evolution of the Gig Economy
................8

Subchapter 1.3: Common Misconceptions About the Gig
Economy.................9

Defining the Gig Economy 10

History and Evolution of the Gig Economy................11

Common Misconceptions About the Gig Economy 12

"Gig work is only for people who can't find traditional
employment." 13
"Gig work is unstable and unreliable."................13
"Gig workers don't receive benefits." 14
"Gig work is low skilled and low paying."................14

**Chapter 2: Advantages and Challenges of Working in the
Gig Economy**................15

Subchapter 2.1: Benefits of the Gig Economy 15

Subchapter 2.2: Potential Challenges in the Gig Economy
................16

Subchapter 2.3: Overcoming Limitations in the Gig
Economy 17

Benefits of the Gig Economy 18

Potential Challenges in the Gig Economy................20

Instability................20

Isolation...21

Lack of Benefits 21

Finding Work 22

Unclear Expectations...22

Subchapter 2.3: Overcoming Limitations in the Gig Economy **23**

Chapter 3: Identifying Your Skills and Opportunities 25

Subchapter 3.1: Evaluating Your Skills and Interests.......25

Subchapter 3.2: Finding Profitable Gigs...........................26

Subchapter 3.3: Researching Market Demand and Trends **27**

Evaluating Your Skills and Interests 28

Finding Profitable Gigs 29

Chapter 3: Identifying Your Skills and Opportunities 31

Subchapter 3.3: Researching Market Demand and Trends...31

Chapter 4: Building Your Personal Brand 33

Subchapter 4.1: Importance of Branding in the Gig Economy 33

Subchapter 4.2: Enhancing Your Online Presence 34

Subchapter 4.3: Showcasing Your Work and Portfolio 35

Importance of Branding in the Gig Economy...................36

Enhancing Your Online Presence 37

1. Build a professional website..38

2. Optimize your social media profiles 38

3. Create a strong portfolio 39

4. Utilize search engine optimization (SEO) 39

Showcasing Your Work and Portfolio 40

Chapter 5: Establishing Multiple Income Streams 42

Subchapter 5.1: Advantages of Having Multiple Income Streams..42

Subchapter 5.2: Diversifying Your Income Sources 43

Subchapter 5.3: Balancing Multiple Gigs and Projects 44

Advantages of Having Multiple Income Streams.............45

Subchapter 5.2: Diversifying Your Income Sources 46
1. Offer a mix of one-time and recurring gigs 47
2. Explore new industries and niches 48
3. Build passive income streams 48
4. Maximize your earnings from existing gigs 49

Subchapter 5.3: Balancing Multiple Gigs and Projects 50
1. Prioritize Your Tasks 50
2. Use Time Management Techniques 51
3. Keep Everything Organized 51
4. Set Realistic Expectations...51
5. Take Breaks 52

Chapter 6: Managing Your Finances 53

Subchapter 6.1: Creating a Budget 53

Subchapter 6.2: Tracking Your Income and Expenses......54

Subchapter 6.3: Saving and Investing in the Gig Economy
....55

Creating a Budget..56

Tracking Your Income and Expenses...............................58

Saving and Investing in the Gig Economy........................59

4

The Gig Economy: How to Build a Career Around Flexible Work and Multiple Income Streams............................**61**

Chapter 7: Staying Motivated and Productive **61**

Dealing with Isolation and Burnout.......................................62

Establishing a Routine and Schedule...................................63

Maximizing Efficiency and Time Management.....................63

Dealing with Isolation and Burnout **64**

Establishing a Routine and Schedule **66**

Subchapter 7.3: Maximizing Efficiency and Time Management **67**

1. Use a project management tool.......................................68

2. Set realistic deadlines..68

3. Prioritize your work..68

4. Use time-blocking...69

5. Minimize distractions 69

6. Take breaks 70

Thriving in the Future of Work **70**

Predictions and Trends in the Gig Economy...................**71**

Preparing for Changes and Adaptation...........................**72**

Creating a Sustainable and Successful Career in the Gig Economy **73**

Predictions and Trends in the Gig Economy...................**74**

1. Continued growth in the gig economy 74

2. Increased use of artificial intelligence 74

3. Emphasis on diversity and inclusivity 75

4. Expansion into new industries 75

5. Increase in virtual work 76

Subchapter 8.2: Preparing for Changes and Adaptation..76

Chapter 1: Understanding the Gig Economy

The gig economy refers to a growing trend in which people work as independent contractors or freelancers, rather than permanent employees. The term "gig" originally referred to the music industry, where performers were hired for single shows or engagements. However, it has since expanded to include any type of temporary or project-based work.

SUBCHAPTER 1.1: DEFINING THE GIG ECONOMY

The gig economy is characterized by short-term contracts or freelance work. Workers in the gig economy are typically paid on a per-gig basis, rather than receiving a regular salary or wage. This type of work can include anything from driving for a ride-sharing service to writing articles for blogs and websites.

SUBCHAPTER 1.2: HISTORY AND EVOLUTION OF THE GIG ECONOMY

The gig economy has been growing steadily over the past few decades, especially with the rise of the internet and digital technology. The first gig economy platform, Craigslist, was launched in 1995, with other platforms like Uber, Airbnb, and TaskRabbit following in the early 2000s. One of the main events that accelerated the growth of the gig economy was the 2008 financial crisis. Many people who had lost their jobs turned to gig work as a way to make ends meet. Today, the gig economy is not just a side hustle for some; it's a full-time career choice.

SUBCHAPTER 1.3: COMMON MISCONCEPTIONS ABOUT THE GIG ECONOMY

There are several misconceptions about the gig economy that should be addressed. One is the idea that gig work is just a temporary solution for people who can't find "real" jobs. In reality, many people choose to work in the gig economy because of the flexibility and autonomy it offers. Another misconception is that gig work is unstable and unreliable. While it's true that gig workers don't have the same job security as traditional employees, many have found ways to create a stable income by diversifying their income streams and building long-term relationships with clients. Overall, the gig economy is a rapidly growing and evolving field that offers both opportunities and challenges. Understanding its history, definition, and common misconceptions is an important first step in building a successful career in this field.

DEFINING THE GIG ECONOMY

The gig economy is a relatively new term that has gained popularity in recent years. Simply put, it refers to a labor market where temporary or freelance jobs are the norm, rather than traditional full-time employment. Gigs can be short-term or long-term and can range from simple, one-time tasks to complex, ongoing projects. Workers in the gig economy are often referred to as "gig workers" or "independent contractors". This type of employment offers greater flexibility and autonomy for workers, as well as the ability to work on a variety of projects and with multiple clients. Additionally, companies can benefit from the gig economy by reducing their fixed labor costs and accessing a wider pool of talent. However, this flexible and agile work arrangement can also create uncertainties, such as irregular income, lack of benefits, and job security concerns. It is essential to be well-informed about the gig economy and understand its unique dynamics to make the most of the opportunities available.

HISTORY AND EVOLUTION OF THE GIG ECONOMY

The concept of "gig work" has been around for centuries, but the term "gig economy" is a relatively recent invention. The roots of the modern gig economy can be traced back to the 2008 financial crisis, which caused widespread layoffs throughout many industries and a shift towards more flexible, independent work arrangements. However, the gig economy truly began to take shape with the rise of platforms like Uber, Lyft, and Postmates, which enabled individual contractors to earn income on their own schedules by providing on-demand services. These companies used technology to facilitate the matching of consumers with service providers, creating a new market for gig work. The gig economy has continued to evolve and expand, with new players entering the market and new niches emerging. Today, more and more workers are turning to freelancing and gig work as a way to make ends meet, supplement their income, or pursue their passions. Although the gig economy presents new freedoms and opportunities for workers, it also raises some concerns surrounding worker protections, benefits, and job security. As the gig economy continues to grow and evolve, it's up to policymakers, businesses, and workers themselves to find ways to ensure that all individuals have access to fair and sustainable work opportunities.

COMMON MISCONCEPTIONS ABOUT THE GIG ECONOMY

There are many misconceptions about the gig economy that can discourage people from pursuing this type of work. Let's explore and debunk some of these common misconceptions:

"Gig work is only for people who can't find traditional employment."

This is not true. Many gig workers intentionally choose this type of work because it offers more flexibility, autonomy, and income potential than traditional employment. In fact, some highly skilled individuals, such as software engineers and graphic designers, may be able to earn significantly more as gig workers than they could in a traditional job.

"Gig work is unstable and unreliable."

While it's true that gig work doesn't offer the same level of job security as traditional employment, it can be just as reliable if you take a strategic approach. One way to increase your stability as a gig worker is to diversify your income streams and build long-term relationships with clients. Additionally, many gig workers appreciate the constant flow of new projects and opportunities, which can provide a sense of excitement and motivation.

"Gig workers don't receive benefits."

It's true that gig workers aren't typically offered traditional employee benefits, such as healthcare and retirement plans. However, many gig platforms, such as Uber and Lyft, offer some form of benefits to their workers. Additionally, gig workers can take advantage of individual health insurance plans and self-directed retirement accounts.

"Gig work is low skilled and low paying."

While there certainly are low-skilled and low-paying gig jobs available, there are also many high-skilled and high-paying gigs as well. In fact, some gig workers can earn six-figure incomes or more by leveraging their expertise and experience in a certain field.

The key is to identify your unique skills and offerings, and then market yourself effectively to potential clients. By understanding and debunking these common misconceptions about the gig economy, you can better assess whether this type of work is a good fit for you, and confidently pursue new opportunities.

Chapter 2: Advantages and Challenges of Working in the Gig Economy

SUBCHAPTER 2.1: BENEFITS OF THE GIG ECONOMY

The gig economy offers numerous advantages to those who are willing to take the plunge. One of the most significant an individual can experience is flexibility. The gig economy allows workers to create their schedules, which means they can tailor their work hours to meet their specific needs. This flexibility can come in handy when handling personal responsibilities like caring for children or elderly relatives. Another benefit of the gig economy is the chance to pursue multiple income streams. Gig workers are not confined to any particular industry or niche. Hence, they can take up different gigs that suit their interests and unique skill set. Gig work is also an excellent way for individuals to gain valuable work experience that they can leverage in the future. The diverse set of people and companies encountered by gig workers provides numerous opportunities to learn new skills and stay up to date with emerging trends.

SUBCHAPTER 2.2: POTENTIAL CHALLENGES IN THE GIG ECONOMY

Like any work setup, working in a gig economy comes with its share of difficulties. One of the most significant challenges is the absence of benefits, such as paid time off, healthcare, and retirement benefits. Gig workers are typically independent contractors and are, therefore, not entitled to the benefits that most full-time employees receive. Another potential challenge is the instability of work in the gig economy. Some gigs don't last long, meaning that a worker's income source can dry up in an instant. This unpredictability can make it difficult to plan for the future and stay financially stable. Finally, working alone and managing multiple gigs and clients can be incredibly overwhelming, mentally and physically. Workers in the gig economy need to carefully balance their workload and take the time to care for themselves and their well-being.

SUBCHAPTER 2.3: OVERCOMING LIMITATIONS IN THE GIG ECONOMY

While there are benefits to working in the gig economy, it's essential to understand and mitigate potential challenges. One way to surmount the absence of benefits is by taking advantage of those available in your locality, such as publicly available healthcare or retirement solutions. Having a financial plan that takes the unpredictability of work into account is also critical in managing the possibility of losing a gig or facing a dry spell. Creating a cushion fund for emergencies or considering part-time work alongside your gigs can help supplement your income. Finally, self-care is of utmost importance in the gig economy. Freelancers must learn to manage their workload and maintain a healthy work-life balance to avoid burnout and isolation. Setting clear boundaries, taking breaks, and working conventional hours can help mitigate these issues and sustain a productive, fulfilling career in the gig economy.

BENEFITS OF THE GIG ECONOMY

There are numerous benefits to working in the gig economy that make it an attractive option for many people. One of the most significant advantages is the flexibility it offers. Unlike traditional jobs, which often require a set schedule and routine, gig work allows you to set your own hours and work at your own pace. This means that you can work around other commitments, such as family obligations or personal interests, and still earn an income. Another benefit of the gig economy is the variety of opportunities available. With so many different types of gigs, from writing and graphic design to driving and caregiving, there is something for everyone. This means that you can pursue work that aligns with your skills and interests, and even experiment with new types of work to see what you enjoy. The gig economy also provides the opportunity to earn more money than in traditional jobs. With multiple income streams, you can potentially earn more than you would in a single job, especially if you are able to leverage your skills and expertise to command higher rates. Additionally, you may be able to take advantage of tax write-offs and deductions for home office expenses and business-related travel. Finally, the gig economy offers a sense of independence and control over your career. Instead of being at the mercy of a single employer or company, you have the ability to pursue work that aligns with your values and goals. This can lead to greater job satisfaction and a sense of fulfillment in your work. Overall, the gig economy provides a range of benefits that make it an attractive choice for those seeking flexibility, variety, financial opportunity, and independence in their work.

POTENTIAL CHALLENGES IN THE GIG ECONOMY

Working in the gig economy has its fair share of challenges. As a gig worker, you may face obstacles that traditional employees do not. Here are some common challenges to be aware of:

Instability

The gig economy is known for its unpredictability. As a gig worker, you are not guaranteed a steady income or job security. Some months, you may have more work than you can handle, while other months, you may struggle to make ends meet. This instability can cause stress and anxiety, which can be difficult to manage.

Isolation

Many gig workers work from home or remotely. While this provides flexibility and freedom, it can also be isolating. Without coworkers or a physical office, it can be challenging to form social connections. It is important to prioritize social interactions and find ways to connect with others, even if it is virtually.

Lack of Benefits

Traditional employees often receive benefits such as health insurance, retirement plans, and paid time off. As a gig worker, you are typically responsible for providing your own benefits. This can be costly and time-consuming to research and manage. It is important to budget and plan for these expenses as part of your overall financial plan.

Finding Work

As a gig worker, you are responsible for finding your own work. This means constantly searching for new gigs and clients, which can be time-consuming and competitive. Building a strong network and marketing your skills is critical to staying competitive and finding consistent work.

Unclear Expectations

As a gig worker, you may work with clients who have unclear expectations. This can lead to confusion and frustration on both sides. To avoid miscommunication, it is important to establish clear expectations and boundaries from the beginning of the project. This includes discussing timelines, deliverables, and payment terms. It is important to acknowledge these potential challenges and proactively address them to ensure success in the gig economy. By being aware of these obstacles and developing strategies to overcome them, gig workers can strive for a fulfilling and sustainable career.

SUBCHAPTER 2.3: OVERCOMING LIMITATIONS IN THE GIG ECONOMY

Working in the gig economy offers many benefits, but like any work situation, there are also challenges that must be addressed. In this subchapter, we will discuss some of the common limitations that come with gig work and strategies you can use to overcome them. One of the major limitations of gig work is the lack of job security and stability. Without a traditional employer, your income sources can be unpredictable and subject to change. To overcome this, it's important to diversify your income streams by pursuing a variety of gigs and projects. This can help to protect against fluctuations in demand for any one particular service or skill. Another limitation is the potential for isolation and loneliness. Without the structure of a traditional workplace, you may miss out on the social connections and networking opportunities that come with it. To counteract this, consider joining coworking spaces or attending industry events to meet other professionals working in your field. This can help you to build relationships and stay connected with others in your industry. Finally, one of the biggest limitations of gig work is the lack of benefits and protections that come with traditional employment, such as healthcare, retirement options, and workers' compensation. To address this issue, it's essential to research and understand your options for obtaining these benefits and protections on your own, through organizations such as a healthcare exchange or freelancer's union. Additionally, be sure to set aside funds for taxes and other expenses that may not be automatically deducted from your paychecks. In conclusion, the gig economy offers many opportunities for flexible work and multiple income streams, but it also comes with its own set of limitations. By diversifying your income sources, building relationships with other professionals, and being proactive about obtaining benefits and protections, you can overcome these limitations and succeed in the gig economy.

Chapter 3: Identifying Your Skills and Opportunities

SUBCHAPTER 3.1: EVALUATING YOUR SKILLS AND INTERESTS

Your skills and interests are the foundation of your success in the gig economy. To find the right opportunities, you need to have a clear understanding of your strengths and passions. Take some time to reflect on your skills and think about the areas where you excel. If you're not sure where to start, consider taking online assessments or talking to colleagues or friends who can provide honest feedback. Identifying your unique talents can help you stand out in a crowded marketplace. Your interests are just as important as your skills. Look for gigs that align with your passions and hobbies. This will not only make your work more enjoyable, but also increase your motivation and creativity.

SUBCHAPTER 3.2: FINDING PROFITABLE GIGS

Once you've identified your skills and interests, it's time to start looking for gigs that can generate income. You can find opportunities through online platforms like Upwork, Freelancer, and Fiverr, or through networking and referrals. When evaluating gigs, consider factors such as the pay rate, the time commitment, and the potential for repeat business. Look for opportunities that allow you to leverage your existing skills and expertise while also learning new ones. Keep in mind that not all gigs are created equal. Some may provide a steady stream of income, while others may be more sporadic. It's important to create a diverse portfolio of gigs to ensure a stable income stream.

SUBCHAPTER 3.3: RESEARCHING MARKET DEMAND AND TRENDS

As you evaluate potential gigs, it's important to research market demand and trends. This can help you identify areas where there is a high need for your skills and expertise. Look for industries that are experiencing growth and that have a high demand for freelance or contract work. Keep an eye on emerging technologies and tools that may be relevant to your gig work. Another useful strategy is to analyze your competition. Look at what other freelancers or contractors are offering and identify areas where you can differentiate yourself. This can help you craft a unique value proposition that sets you apart from the crowd.

EVALUATING YOUR SKILLS AND INTERESTS

When it comes to building a successful career in the gig economy, it's important to start by evaluating your skills and interests. This will help you identify what type of work you're best suited for and give you a better idea of what types of gigs you should be pursuing. First, take a look at your existing skills. What are you good at? What unique talents do you have? Make a list of your skills and experience, no matter how small or seemingly inconsequential. It's important to consider all possibilities and think outside the box. Next, consider your interests. What do you enjoy doing in your free time? What hobbies do you have? By aligning your work with your passions, you're more likely to find fulfillment and longevity in your gig career. Finally, think about how your skills and interests can be monetized. Are there any specific niches or industries where your skills could be in high demand? Do some market research to identify potential areas for your services. Remember, when evaluating your skills and interests, it's important to be honest with yourself and realistic about what you can offer. Don't overlook your strengths, but also be aware of any weaknesses or areas where you may need to improve. By doing so, you'll be better equipped to find success in the gig economy.

FINDING PROFITABLE GIGS

When it comes to working in the gig economy, finding profitable gigs is essential for building a sustainable career. One of the best ways to find gigs is by leveraging online platforms that connect freelancers with clients. Sites like Upwork, Fiverr, and Freelancer make it easy to create a profile and start bidding on projects that match your skills and interests. These platforms allow you to set your own rates and choose which projects to take on, giving you a high degree of flexibility and control over your work. Another way to find profitable gigs is by networking with other professionals in your industry. Joining online communities and attending networking events can help you connect with potential clients and build relationships that can lead to future opportunities. It's also important to keep an eye out for emerging trends and market demands. As the gig economy continues to evolve, new opportunities are constantly arising in areas like virtual assistance, social media management, and content creation. By staying up-to-date on these trends and positioning yourself as an expert in your niche, you can attract high-paying clients and build a loyal customer base. Ultimately, finding profitable gigs in the gig economy requires a combination of strategy, networking, and adaptability. By staying focused on your goals and being proactive in seeking out new opportunities, you can build a successful and fulfilling career as a gig worker.

CHAPTER 3: IDENTIFYING YOUR SKILLS AND OPPORTUNITIES

Subchapter 3.3: Researching Market Demand and Trends

One of the keys to succeeding in the gig economy is keeping up with market demand and industry trends. To effectively position yourself for success, you need to have a good understanding of which skills are in demand, where businesses are focusing their efforts, and where the economy is heading. By staying up-to-date on market demand and trends, you can better identify which gigs to pursue and how to best market your skills and services. To begin researching market demand and trends, start by looking at job boards and freelance websites to see which types of gigs are in high demand. You can also talk to other freelancers or professionals in your industry to get a sense of where the industry is headed. Additionally, consider subscribing to industry publications and attending industry events, such as conferences or webinars, to learn more about emerging trends and new innovations. When researching market demand and trends, it's also important to pay attention to broader economic and societal factors, such as changes in technology, shifts in consumer behavior, and advancements in artificial intelligence. By keeping up with these larger trends, you can better position yourself for long-term success in the gig economy. Ultimately, by staying up-to-date on market demand and trends, you can better understand where to focus your efforts and how to adapt to changing economic conditions and industry developments. This can help you build a sustainable and successful career in the gig economy that can provide flexibility and financial stability.

Chapter 4: Building Your Personal Brand

SUBCHAPTER 4.1: IMPORTANCE OF BRANDING IN THE GIG ECONOMY

In today's gig economy, it's not enough to just have a great skill set. You need to stand out from the crowd and make a name for yourself. This is where building a strong personal brand comes into play. Your personal brand is what sets you apart from other gig workers and helps potential clients and customers understand what you bring to the table. One of the biggest benefits of having a strong personal brand is that it can help you attract the right kind of clients and projects. By crafting a clear and compelling message about who you are, what you do and why you do it, you can position yourself as an expert in your field, making it more likely that people will seek you out for work.

SUBCHAPTER 4.2: ENHANCING YOUR ONLINE PRESENCE

In order to build a strong personal brand in the gig economy, it's important to have a strong online presence. This doesn't just mean having a website or a social media profile, but rather a cohesive and consistent online presence across all platforms. Start by choosing a few key platforms that align with the type of work you're doing, and focus on building out those profiles with high-quality content and visuals. This could include everything from photos of your work to blog posts about industry trends and insights. Remember to keep everything on-brand and cohesive, so that your potential clients and customers get a clear sense of who you are and what you can offer them.

SUBCHAPTER 4.3:
SHOWCASING YOUR WORK
AND PORTFOLIO

Another important piece of building your personal brand is showcasing your work and portfolio. As a gig worker, your work will speak for itself, and it's important to have a way to show it off to potential clients and customers. Start by creating a portfolio of your best work that can be easily shared online and offline. This could be in the form of a website, a PDF document, or even a physical portfolio that you can bring to meetings. Whatever format you choose, make sure it's easy to navigate and showcases your skills and expertise. Remember, building your personal brand is an ongoing process. It takes time and effort to craft a clear and compelling message, and to establish a strong online presence. But with the right approach, you can set yourself apart from the competition and build a successful career in the gig economy.

IMPORTANCE OF BRANDING IN THE GIG ECONOMY

In the competitive world of the gig economy, it's not enough to simply have the skills necessary to perform a job. Building a strong personal brand is crucial in order to stand out from the crowd and attract potential clients and customers. Your personal brand is a combination of your skills, experience, personality, and reputation. It's what sets you apart from others in your field and makes you memorable to potential clients. By investing time and effort into developing your personal brand, you'll be able to command higher rates and attract more lucrative opportunities. Branding in the gig economy goes beyond just having a logo or catchy tagline. It's about cultivating a unique identity that resonates with your target audience and communicates the value you bring to the table. This can include creating a visually appealing website or portfolio, crafting a compelling bio or mission statement, and consistently producing high-quality work that aligns with your brand values. A strong personal brand can also help you build credibility and trust with potential clients, as it demonstrates your professionalism, expertise, and commitment to quality. In today's digital age, having a strong online presence is essential, as many clients and customers will look you up online before deciding to work with you. By cultivating a strong personal brand, you'll be able to make a positive impression and demonstrate your expertise before even meeting in person. In summary, branding is a critical component of success in the gig economy. By investing time and effort in developing a strong personal brand, you'll be able to stand out from the competition, attract high-paying clients and customers, and build a successful and sustainable career.

ENHANCING YOUR ONLINE PRESENCE

In the gig economy, having a strong online presence is crucial to attracting clients and finding new opportunities. Your online presence not only represents your brand but also serves as a platform to showcase your skills, experience, and portfolio. Here are some tips to enhance your online presence:

1. Build a professional website

Having a professional website can make a huge impact on potential clients. It provides them with a clear way to learn about your services, skills, and experience. Make sure your website is visually appealing, easy to navigate, and mobile-friendly. Including testimonials from past clients, and a clear call-to-action for visitors can also help you convert potential leads into actual clients.

2. Optimize your social media profiles

Social media platforms like LinkedIn, Twitter, and Instagram provide an avenue to showcase your work, connect with peers in your industry, and promote your services. Make sure your profiles are complete, up-to-date, and reflect your personal brand. It's also important to engage with your followers and share valuable content on a regular basis.

3. Create a strong portfolio

Whether you're a writer, designer, or photographer, having a portfolio to showcase your work is crucial to attracting new clients. Consider adding samples of your best work on your website, social media profiles, and other relevant platforms. Be sure to include detailed descriptions that highlight your skills and the value you can offer to potential clients.

4. Utilize search engine optimization (SEO)

Search engine optimization (SEO) is the process of improving your website's visibility on search engines like Google. By optimizing your website and content with relevant keywords related to your services, you can increase your chances of being found by potential clients. Consider hiring an SEO specialist or taking an online course to learn more about how to optimize your website. By following these tips, you can create a strong online presence that showcases your skills, experience, and value in the gig economy. Remember, your online presence is a reflection of your personal brand and can make all the difference in attracting new clients and building a successful career.

SHOWCASING YOUR WORK AND PORTFOLIO

In the gig economy, potential clients want to see your previous work to understand what type of quality and style they can expect from you. This means that it's crucial to have a portfolio to showcase your best work and demonstrate your skills to potential clients. When creating your portfolio, it's important to choose your best work, and ensure that your portfolio reflects the type of work you want to attract. Make sure to include both completed projects and work in progress, as it demonstrates your experience in delivering high-quality work. There are several platforms where you can host your portfolio, such as Behance, Dribbble, and WordPress. Make sure to include a professional-looking profile picture, a brief bio, and your contact information. To make your portfolio stand out, you can identify a specific niche where you excel and specialize in that area. You can also use your portfolio to tell a story about your professional journey, showcasing growth and experience over time. If possible, include before-and-after examples or testimonials from satisfied clients to provide social proof of your work. Don't be afraid to showcase your personality in your portfolio. Clients are looking for someone they can trust and work comfortably with, and being authentic and personable can set you apart from competitors. Remember, a well-polished portfolio can be the difference between securing a lucrative project and losing out to a competitor. Spend time crafting your portfolio and make sure it represents your best work and personality.

Chapter 5: Establishing Multiple Income Streams

SUBCHAPTER 5.1: ADVANTAGES OF HAVING MULTIPLE INCOME STREAMS

Having multiple income streams is an essential aspect of building a successful career in the gig economy. By diversifying your income sources, you can increase your earning potential and reduce the risk of relying on a single gig or client. There are several advantages to having multiple income streams. First and foremost, it allows you to generate more revenue and increase your overall income. This can provide financial security and stability, which is especially important when dealing with the volatility of the gig economy. Furthermore, having multiple income streams can also provide flexibility and autonomy. You're not tied to a single employer or a specific schedule, which allows you to take on different jobs and projects that align with your skills and interests. This flexibility can also provide a sense of control over your career and lifestyle, which can lead to greater overall satisfaction.

SUBCHAPTER 5.2: DIVERSIFYING YOUR INCOME SOURCES

Diversifying your income sources means identifying different types of gigs or projects that you can work on to generate revenue. This can include freelance work, consulting, teaching, and even creating and selling your own products or services. To diversify your income sources, you need to evaluate your skills and interests and determine what types of jobs or projects you're best suited for. This may require doing some research and networking, reaching out to potential clients or employers, and building a portfolio that showcases your work and skills. It's important to note that diversifying your income sources doesn't mean taking on too many gigs or projects that it becomes overwhelming and affects the quality of your work. Instead, it's about finding a balance that enables you to generate revenue and maintain a reasonable workload.

SUBCHAPTER 5.3: BALANCING MULTIPLE GIGS AND PROJECTS

Balancing multiple gigs and projects can be challenging, but it's essential to maintain productivity and avoid burnout. To balance your workload, you need to prioritize your tasks and manage your time effectively. One tip is to create a schedule or planner where you can track your different gigs and projects, set deadlines and goals, and allocate your time accordingly. You can also consider outsourcing or delegating some tasks, such as administrative work or marketing, to free up more time for the core elements of your work. It's also essential to take breaks and prioritize self-care to avoid burnout. This may include taking regular breaks, practicing mindfulness or meditation, or engaging in physical activity. By taking care of yourself, you'll be better equipped to manage your workload and maintain productivity across your multiple income streams.

ADVANTAGES OF HAVING MULTIPLE INCOME STREAMS

In the gig economy, having multiple income streams can provide numerous advantages. First and foremost, it can offer greater financial stability as it allows you to diversify your income sources. This means that if one gig slows down or disappears altogether, you still have other sources of income to rely on. Additionally, having multiple income streams can lead to increased earning potential. By working on different gigs and projects simultaneously, you can increase your total earnings compared to if you were working on just one source of income. Moreover, having multiple income streams can provide more flexibility in terms of work schedule. You can choose to work on multiple projects at different times of the day, giving you greater control over your work-life balance. Finally, having multiple income streams can offer opportunities for personal and professional growth. By working on different projects, you can develop new skills and experiences that can benefit your overall career. Overall, the advantages of having multiple income streams in the gig economy are clear. It can provide financial stability, increased earning potential, flexibility, and opportunities for personal and professional growth.

SUBCHAPTER 5.2: DIVERSIFYING YOUR INCOME SOURCES

One of the key principles of building a successful career in the gig economy is diversifying your income sources. Relying on a single income stream can be risky, especially since many gigs may be temporary or subject to market fluctuations. By spreading your income across several different streams, you can create a more stable and sustainable income that is less vulnerable to unexpected changes. There are many ways you can diversify your income in the gig economy. Some gig workers choose to pursue multiple different gigs in different industries, while others may focus on building passive income streams through investments or digital products. Here are some strategies to consider:

1. Offer a mix of one-time and recurring gigs

One way to diversify your income is to offer a mix of both one-time projects and recurring gigs. This can help ensure that you have a steady flow of income even when you are between projects or experiencing a slow period. Recurring gigs can also help you build strong relationships with clients and ensure a regular income stream.

2. Explore new industries and niches

Another way to diversify your income is to explore new industries and niches. This can help you tap into new markets and opportunities, and may also help you expand your skills and expertise. Keep an eye on emerging trends and technologies in your field, and be willing to experiment with new types of gigs and projects.

3. Build passive income streams

Passive income streams can help you generate income even when you are not working, and can provide a valuable source of financial stability. Some examples of passive income streams may include investing in stocks or real estate, building a digital product like an e-book or online course, or developing a mobile app.

4. Maximize your earnings from existing gigs

Finally, it's important to maximize your earnings from existing gigs by upselling to current clients and identifying new revenue streams. For example, you could offer additional services beyond your core gig offering, or consider offering a premium package that includes additional features or services. Diversifying your income sources is an important step towards building a successful career in the gig economy. By exploring new industries and niches, building passive income streams, and maximizing your earnings from existing gigs, you can create a more stable and sustainable income that can help you thrive in the competitive world of gig work.

SUBCHAPTER 5.3: BALANCING MULTIPLE GIGS AND PROJECTS

When you're working in the gig economy, it's common to have multiple gigs and projects on the go at the same time. While this can be exciting and financially rewarding, it can also be challenging to balance everything effectively. Here are some tips for managing multiple gigs and projects:

1. Prioritize Your Tasks

One of the most important things you can do to manage multiple gigs and projects is to prioritize your tasks. Determine which tasks are most important and urgent and make sure you tackle those first. This will ensure that you're meeting deadlines and delivering quality work on time.

2. Use Time Management Techniques

Time management techniques can be incredibly helpful when it comes to managing multiple gigs and projects. Consider using the Pomodoro Technique, which involves working in focused, 25-minute chunks with short breaks in between. This can help you stay focused and increase your productivity.

3. Keep Everything Organized

When you're juggling multiple gigs and projects, it's essential to keep everything organized. Use apps like Trello or Asana to track your tasks and deadlines, and make sure all your important documents, files, and communications are stored in one place.

4. Set Realistic Expectations

It can be tempting to take on more gigs and projects than you can realistically handle, but this can quickly lead to burnout and poor quality work. Be honest with yourself and with your clients about what you can and can't manage, and don't be afraid to say no to work if it's too much to handle.

5. Take Breaks

When you're working on multiple gigs and projects, it can be challenging to take breaks, but it's essential for your mental and physical health. Make sure you schedule downtime into your day, whether it's a quick walk outside or a yoga session. Taking a break can help you recharge and come back to your work with a fresh perspective. By prioritizing your tasks, using time management techniques, staying organized, setting realistic expectations, and taking breaks, you can successfully balance multiple gigs and projects in the gig economy. It may take some time and practice to find the right balance, but with persistence and determination, you can create a sustainable and rewarding career.

Chapter 6: Managing Your Finances

Finances can be a daunting topic, especially when working in the gig economy where income can fluctuate. However, with proper management, it is possible to create stability and achieve financial success. In this chapter, we will explore the steps you can take to manage your finances effectively.

SUBCHAPTER 6.1: CREATING A BUDGET

Creating a budget is the first step in managing your finances. A budget allows you to track your income and expenses and helps you identify areas where you can cut back or save. Start by calculating your monthly income from all your gigs and projects. Then, list out your recurring expenses such as rent/mortgage, utilities, transportation, groceries, and any debt payments. Be sure to also include any irregular expenses like taxes, insurance, or unexpected expenses. Once you have a clear picture of your income and expenses, you can identify areas where you can cut back or allocate more funds. It's essential to be realistic and flexible with your budget. Remember, your income may vary from month to month, so be prepared to adjust your budget accordingly.

SUBCHAPTER 6.2: TRACKING YOUR INCOME AND EXPENSES

Tracking your income and expenses is crucial to understand where your money is going and to stay within your budget. There are many tools available to help you with this, from mobile apps to spreadsheets. Consider linking your bank account to an app like Mint or YNAB, which will track your spending automatically and allow you to visually see where your money is going. Alternatively, you can use a spreadsheet to manually track your income and expenses daily. It's essential to stay on top of your finances and regularly review your spending to make sure you're staying within your budget. It's also essential to keep track of your taxes and set aside funds for tax payments.

SUBCHAPTER 6.3: SAVING AND INVESTING IN THE GIG ECONOMY

Saving and investing should be a part of any good financial plan. Start by building an emergency fund to cover unexpected expenses or dips in income. A good rule of thumb is to save at least 3-6 months of expenses. Once you have an emergency fund, consider contributing to a retirement account. Many gig workers may not have access to a traditional employer-sponsored retirement plan, but options like Individual Retirement Accounts (IRAs) and Simplified Employee Pension (SEP) plans are available and can provide tax benefits while helping to secure your financial future. Investing can also be a wise way to build long-term wealth. Educate yourself on different investment options and consider consulting with a financial advisor to create a plan that aligns with your goals and risk tolerance. Managing your finances can be overwhelming, but taking these steps can provide peace of mind and financial stability. Remember to regularly review and adjust your budget and track your income and expenses. Build an emergency fund and consider saving and investing for the future.

CREATING A BUDGET

One of the most important aspects of success in the gig economy is careful financial planning. One of the first steps in this process is creating a budget. A budget allows you to track your expenses and income, identify areas for improvement and prioritize your spending. To create a budget, start by analyzing your income sources and expenses. Consider fixed expenses, such as rent or mortgage payments, car payments, and utility bills. These expenses are typically the same amount each month. You should also consider variable expenses, such as groceries, entertainment, and transportation. Once you have identified your expenses, it's important to compare them to your income. If your expenses exceed your income, you'll need to make changes to your spending habits or find additional sources of income. On the other hand, if your income exceeds your expenses, it's important to set aside some of that money for emergencies or unexpected expenses. Creating a budget may feel overwhelming at first, but there are many tools and resources available to help. Online tools, such as budgeting apps or spreadsheets can be helpful. Additionally, many financial experts recommend setting up automatic payments for bills and expenses to help keep your finances organized and on track. By creating a budget, you'll have a clearer understanding of your financial situation and be better prepared to manage your money in the gig economy.

TRACKING YOUR INCOME AND EXPENSES

One of the most important things you can do as a gig worker is to keep track of your income and expenses. Without a solid understanding of your finances, it is impossible to make informed decisions about your career. To begin tracking your income and expenses, you should start by setting up a simple accounting system. This can be as simple as a spreadsheet or as complex as a full accounting software package. Regardless of the system you choose, make sure it is easy to use and that it gives you a clear picture of your financial situation. When tracking your income, make sure you are including all sources of revenue. This includes money earned from gigs, as well as any other income streams you may have. By tracking all of your income, you can get a better sense of how much you are earning overall and where you may need to focus your efforts to increase your earnings. As for expenses, it is important to track all of the costs associated with running your gig economy career. This includes expenses like equipment, software, workspace rental, and business insurance, as well as any other costs you may incur while working. By tracking your expenses, you can get a better sense of where your money is going and where you might be able to cut costs to improve your overall financial situation. Finally, it is important to regularly review your income and expenses to make informed decisions about your career. By understanding exactly how much money you are making and spending, you can adjust your efforts to maximize your income and minimize your expenses, helping you to thrive in the world of gig work.

SAVING AND INVESTING IN THE GIG ECONOMY

With the promising and unpredictable nature of gig work, it's essential to have a solid plan for your finances. While freelancers and gig workers have the advantage of managing their finances, there is also a need to secure their future by saving and investing. Saving money as a freelancer can be a challenge, and it's essential to keep track of your income and expenses thoroughly. Creating a budget can help you plan your finances better and allocate money for essential expenses such as rent, groceries, and utilities. It's also crucial to set aside money for emergencies and unexpected expenses. The gig economy can also offer unique investment opportunities that can grow your money over time. Consider investing in a retirement account or opening an individual retirement account (IRA) to plan for your retirement. Investing in stocks, bonds, real estate, or small businesses can also provide an extra stream of income. Furthermore, it's vital to do your research before investing your money. Understand the risks of different types of investments and consult with a financial advisor to help you make informed decisions. It's also crucial to diversify your investments and not put all your eggs in one basket. Saving and investing can be challenging as a freelancer, but it's necessary for your financial security in the future. By creating a budget, setting aside money for emergencies, and investing wisely, you can secure a successful career in the gig economy.

The Gig Economy: How to Build a Career Around Flexible Work and Multiple Income Streams

CHAPTER 7: STAYING MOTIVATED AND PRODUCTIVE

In the gig economy, it can be challenging to stay motivated and productive, especially when working from home. As discussed earlier in the book, the gig economy can lead to feelings of isolation and burnout. That's why it's essential to establish a routine that promotes both motivation and productivity.

Dealing with Isolation and Burnout

Isolation and burnout are two common issues faced by gig workers. It's easy to become disconnected from the world when working remotely, and the lack of human interaction can lead to mental health problems. Fortunately, there are several ways to deal with isolation and burnout. One way to tackle isolation is by joining online communities or groups related to your gig work. You can share your experiences, ask for advice, and get support from other gig workers facing similar issues. Another effective method is to schedule regular face-to-face meetings with clients, colleagues, or business partners. These interactions can be motivational and provide a much-needed break from working alone. Burnout occurs when you're working too hard for too long without taking enough breaks. Over time, this can lead to physical and emotional exhaustion, as well as decreased productivity. The best way to prevent burnout in the gig economy is to set realistic goals and manage your work schedule. Make sure you're taking enough breaks and getting plenty of rest.

Establishing a Routine and Schedule

Working in the gig economy can be extremely flexible, but that flexibility can lead to a lack of structure and routine. To stay motivated and productive, it's important to establish a routine that works for you. One effective approach is to set specific work hours and stick to them. This can help you establish a productive work-life balance and avoid burnout. Another approach is to create a to-do list or schedule each day that outlines your tasks and deadlines. This can help you stay on track and avoid procrastination.

Maximizing Efficiency and Time Management

In the gig economy, time is money. That's why it's essential to maximize efficiency and manage your time effectively. One way to do this is by prioritizing your tasks based on their importance. You can use the Eisenhower matrix to determine which tasks are urgent and important, and which ones can wait. Another way to maximize efficiency is by minimizing distractions. Turn off your phone notifications, close unnecessary tabs on your computer, and avoid social media during work hours. You can also usc productivity apps like Trello or Asana to track your progress and collaborate with others. By establishing a routine and schedule, managing your time effectively, and dealing with isolation and burnout, you can stay motivated and productive in the gig economy. Remember, success in the gig economy requires discipline, focus, and dedication.

DEALING WITH ISOLATION AND BURNOUT

Working in the gig economy can provide a lot of freedom and flexibility, but it can also lead to feelings of isolation and burnout. When you work for yourself, you don't have the traditional support network that comes with a traditional job. It's just you and your computer, and sometimes that can be a lonely experience. To combat isolation, it's important to make connections with others in your industry. Attend networking events and meetups, join online communities, and seek out mentorship opportunities. Having a support system can help you feel less alone and give you a sounding board for your ideas and concerns. Burnout is also a common challenge for gig workers, who often feel pressure to take on as much work as possible to make ends meet. It's important to set boundaries for yourself and prioritize self-care. Take breaks throughout the day, exercise regularly, get enough sleep, and make time for hobbies and activities that bring you joy. Remember, you are the most important asset in your business, and your health and well-being should always come first.

ESTABLISHING A ROUTINE AND SCHEDULE

One of the biggest challenges of working in the gig economy is the lack of structure and routine. While flexibility is one of the biggest advantages, it can also lead to procrastination, burnout, and lack of productivity. Establishing a routine and schedule is therefore crucial for success in the gig economy. First and foremost, it's important to identify your most productive hours. Some people work better in the morning, while others are night owls. Most importantly, stick to a consistent schedule so you can maintain a healthy work-life balance. Make sure to set boundaries between work and personal life, and stick to them. Use a planner or calendar to schedule your tasks and deadlines. This can help you prioritize your workload and keep track of what needs to be completed. Utilize technology and apps to your advantage - consider using productivity apps, such as Trello or Asana, to stay on track and organized. Another important aspect is to take regular breaks to avoid burnout. Avoid sitting for long periods of time and consider taking walks or doing a short workout to break up the day. When you're on a break, make sure to fully disconnect from work and recharge your batteries. In conclusion, establishing a routine and schedule is crucial to maintaining motivation, productivity, and success in the gig economy. Find what works best for you, and stick to it. Remember, flexibility is great, but structure and routine are just as important.

SUBCHAPTER 7.3: MAXIMIZING EFFICIENCY AND TIME MANAGEMENT

Working in the gig economy often means managing multiple projects and clients simultaneously. This can quickly become overwhelming if you don't have a system in place to manage your time effectively. Here are some tips to help you maximize your efficiency and time management skills:

1. Use a project management tool

Investing in a project management tool, such as Trello or Asana, can help you keep track of all your projects, deadlines, and deliverables in one place. With these tools, you can break your projects down into manageable tasks, set deadlines, and assign them to specific days on your calendar. This will not only help you stay on track but will also give you a sense of accomplishment as you complete each task.

2. Set realistic deadlines

One of the biggest pitfalls of managing your own schedule is setting unrealistic deadlines. Be honest with yourself about how long a task will take and set a deadline accordingly. This will help you avoid burnout and ensure that you have enough time to complete each project to the best of your ability.

3. Prioritize your work

With so many projects to manage, it's important to prioritize which ones are the most important. You can use the Eisenhower Matrix to help you categorize your tasks based on their importance and urgency. This will help you focus on the tasks that will have the most impact on your business and ensure that you're not wasting time on tasks that don't matter.

4. Use time-blocking

Time-blocking involves scheduling specific blocks of time for certain tasks. This is particularly helpful when you have multiple projects to work on. By blocking out time on your calendar for each project, you can ensure that you're giving each one the attention it deserves and that you're not neglecting any of them.

5. Minimize distractions

Distractions are a major time-waster, particularly when you work from home. To minimize distractions, try turning off your phone notifications, closing unnecessary tabs on your browser, and setting aside dedicated work hours when you're not available to others.

6. Take breaks

Finally, don't forget to take breaks throughout the day. It can be tempting to power through a project without taking a break, but this can actually hinder your productivity in the long run. Taking a short break every hour or so can help you recharge your batteries and come back to your work with a fresh perspective.

Thriving in the Future of Work

The gig economy is a constantly evolving landscape, and as a worker in this field, it's important to stay up-to-date with the latest trends and predictions. In this chapter, we will explore what the future of work might look like, and how you can prepare yourself for potential changes in the market.

PREDICTIONS AND TRENDS IN THE GIG ECONOMY

One trend that we're seeing in the gig economy is the rise of automation and artificial intelligence. As technology continues to advance, more and more jobs are becoming automated, which could potentially lead to a decrease in demand for certain types of gig work. However, it's also possible that new types of job opportunities will emerge as a result of technological advancements. Another trend that is likely to continue in the gig economy is the move towards remote work. With the increasing ease of communication technology, many businesses are starting to feel more comfortable with remote workers. This means that there could be more opportunities for gig workers who are able to work from anywhere and still produce high-quality work.

PREPARING FOR CHANGES AND ADAPTATION

As a gig worker, it's important to be adaptable and versatile. This means that you need to be able to quickly pivot and adjust to changes in the market. One way to do this is to stay up-to-date with the latest trends by reading blogs, attending webinars, and networking with other professionals in your industry. Another important strategy is to diversify your income streams. By having multiple gigs or projects at once, you can ensure that your income is not dependent on any one particular market niche. This can provide a level of security and stability that is not always present in traditional employment.

CREATING A SUSTAINABLE AND SUCCESSFUL CAREER IN THE GIG ECONOMY

The key to success in the gig economy is to focus on building a strong personal brand. This means establishing a reputation for producing high-quality work, being reliable and responsive, and continuously learning and improving your skills. In addition, it's important to manage your finances carefully. Track your income and expenses closely, and always be mindful of your budget. This can help you to weather any financial storms and stay on track towards your long-term goals. Finally, it's important to remember that as a gig worker, you are in charge of your own success. This means taking ownership of your career and working hard to continuously develop your skills and expand your network. With the right mindset and strategies in place, you can thrive in the future of work and build a sustainable and successful career in the gig economy.

PREDICTIONS AND TRENDS IN THE GIG ECONOMY

The gig economy is an ever-evolving landscape, and as technology advances, so do the opportunities and trends within it. Here are some predictions and trends to watch out for in the coming years.

1. Continued growth in the gig economy

According to the Bureau of Labor Statistics, the gig economy is projected to continue to grow over the next decade. This growth is fueled by the desire for flexibility and autonomy in work, especially among millennials and Gen Z.

2. Increased use of artificial intelligence

Artificial intelligence (AI) has already made its way into the gig economy, but its use is expected to increase in the future. AI can be used to match workers with gigs, streamline the hiring process, and even provide virtual assistance to gig workers.

3. Emphasis on diversity and inclusivity

Diversity and inclusivity are becoming a higher priority in the gig economy as more companies recognize the value of having a diverse workforce. This includes not only gender and racial diversity but also diversity in skill sets and backgrounds.

4. Expansion into new industries

The gig economy originally started in industries like ride-sharing and food delivery, but it has since expanded into other sectors like healthcare, education, and finance. This trend is likely to continue as technology continues to advance and new opportunities arise.

5. Increase in virtual work

With COVID-19 pushing more companies to shift to remote work, the gig economy is likely to see an increase in virtual work opportunities. This includes virtual assistants, online tutoring, and remote freelance work. Keeping up with these trends and predictions can help gig workers stay ahead of the curve and maximize their earnings potential in the gig economy.

SUBCHAPTER 8.2: PREPARING FOR CHANGES AND ADAPTATION

In the ever-changing landscape of the gig economy, it's crucial to be prepared for changes and adapt accordingly. As technology continues to advance, new gig platforms emerge, and job markets shift, it's important to stay ahead of the curve and be ready for whatever comes next. One way to prepare for changes in the gig economy is by staying up-to-date with industry news and trends. Subscribe to relevant blogs, newsletters, and social media accounts, and attend industry events and meetups. This will give you valuable insights into emerging opportunities and potential challenges. It's also essential to continue learning and developing your skills. Take courses or workshops that will enhance your abilities and keep you current with industry developments. This will not only make you a more attractive candidate for gigs, but it will also give you the tools to adapt to new situations as they arise. Networking is another vital part of preparing for changes in the gig economy. Build meaningful relationships with other freelancers, entrepreneurs, and industry professionals. This can lead to new opportunities and collaborations, as well as provide a support system for navigating the ups and downs of the gig life. Finally, remember to be flexible and open to new opportunities. Don't get too comfortable with one particular gig or platform, as things can change quickly. Stay nimble and adaptable, and be willing to pivot when necessary to keep your career on track. With the right mindset and approach, you can thrive in the ever-evolving gig economy.

www.ingramcontent.com/pod-product-compliance
Lightning Source LLC
Chambersburg PA
CBHW070454220526
45466CB00004B/1829